# Goodnight Milwaukee

**Written by:** Angie & Ben Buelow

**Illustrated by:** Lindsey Salzwedel

Published by Orange Hat Publishing 2020
ISBN 9-781-64538-132-7

Copyrighted © 2020 by Angie & Ben Buelow
All Rights Reserved
Goodnight Milwaukee
Written by Angie & Ben Buelow
Illustrated by Lindsey Salzwedel

www.orangehatpublishing.com

WiscKids Books
Exploring Wisconsin Together

www.wisckidsbooks.com

In our quest to share the best locations in Wisconsin to say goodnight to: we dedicate this book to all the fans and tourists who can't get enough; and to our friends, family and everyone who calls Milwaukee home.

Goodnight
# Public Market
with your yummy sweet treats.

Goodnight

# Usinger's Sausages

and famous tasty meats.

Goodnight to

# the Domes

and cool rare plants.

Goodnight

# Festival Park

where we sing and dance.

Goodnight
# Bradford Beach
after fun in the sun.

---

Goodnight
# Veterans Park
where we fly kites, play, and run!

Goodnight to
# the sports teams
that keep us on our feet.

---

We're the
# best fans around,
whose spirit can't be beat!

Goodnight to the

# museums

and

# Milwaukee County Zoo.

Goodnight to

# the tigers

and

# elephants

too!

Goodnight

# RiverWalk

where the Bronze Fonz stands.

Goodnight
# Third Ward
and all local bands.

Goodnight

# Kopp's Custard

and the flavors you make.

Goodnight

# State Fair

and the cream puffs you bake!

Goodnight to the suburbs
and all that you do,

**Waukesha,
Wauwatosa,
and Cedarburg**

to name a few.

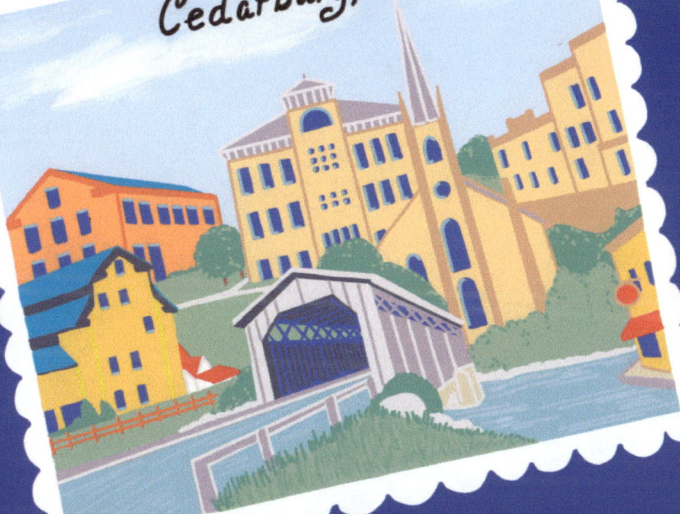

Cedarburg, WI

Waukesha, WI

Wauwatosa, WI

Goodnight

# Brew City

with your rich history.

––––––––––––––––––

You're the brightest in Wisconsin

## and where
## I want to be!

# Fun Facts About
# Milwaukee

Milwaukee is located on Lake Michigan, the second largest of the five Great Lakes, and contains 22,300 square miles of fresh water.

The Public Market does cooking classes with local chefs and some of the most popular cooks in the world.

Usinger's won the competition for best hot dog in North America and supplied 500,000 hot dogs for the Winter Olympics in Salt Lake City. They sold out in 5 days and had to send another 200,000. That's a lot of hot dogs!!!!!

The plants in the Milwaukee Domes are estimated at 3.2 million dollars. HOLY COW!

Festival Park has on average 1.5 million patrons per year.

Milwaukee is proud to be home to over 140 public parks, whose total area consists of 23 square miles!! Lots of places to run and play. Try to visit them all.

Milwaukee Bucks (professional basketball) – 1968 to present
Milwaukee Braves (professional baseball) – 1953-1965
Milwaukee Brewers (professional baseball) – 1970 to present
Milwaukee Torrent (professional soccer) – 2015 to present

The Milwaukee Wave is the oldest soccer team in the US. This indoor soccer team has been around since 1984, and is still going strong today.

There are 22 museums in Milwaukee. The Milwaukee Zoo is one of the top 10 zoos in the country.

There are 50-60 cream puffs sold per minute at the Wisconsin State Fair, with an average of over 400,000 sold in just 11 days!

The Milwaukee Public Museum is home to the largest dinosaur head in the world.

Summerfest is the largest music festival in the world, with around 800,000 visitors and 1,000 performances in 11 days!

The Polar Plunge, where people jump into a frozen Lake Michigan, has been a New Year's tradition since 1916. Brrrrrrrrr!

The Milwaukee RiverWalk is over 3 miles long and home to the Bronze Fonz.

Milwaukee is the largest city in the state of Wisconsin with a population of close to 600,000 in 2020.

Harley Davidson was started by two men, William Harley and Arthur Davidson, in a 10x15 foot shed in Milwaukee.

The wings on the Milwaukee Art Museum close and open every day. If the winds get too high, they close automatically. HOLY COW!!!

Brew City gets its nickname honestly! Milwaukee is home to 3 of the top 5 oldest breweries in the country! Pabst (1844), Blatz (1846), and Old Milwaukee (1849).

# Milwaukee Bucket List

Use the next page to track your amazing adventures!

We'd love to see you! Tag us on social media using:

**#wisckidsadventures** or **#goodnightmilwaukee**

**FB:** @WiscKidsBooks | **Insta:** @wisckids_books

## Milwaukee Public Market

Date_____

## Veterans Park/Bradford Beach

Date_____

## Discovery World

Date_____

## Sporting Event

Date_____

## The Domes

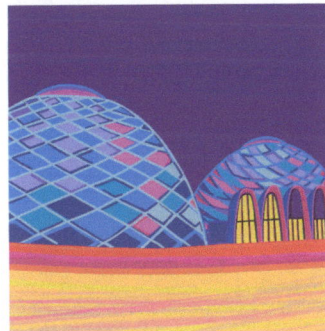

Date_____

## Milwaukee County Zoo

Date_____

## The Third Ward

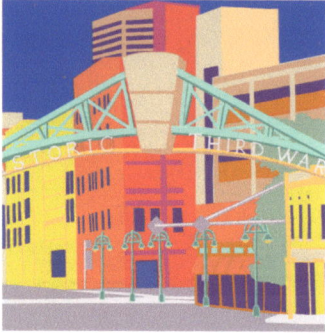

Date_____

## Milwaukee Art Museum

Date_____

## Kopp's Frozen Custard

Date_____

## The Bronze Fonz/Riverwalk

Date_____

## Wisconsin State Fair

Date_____

## Henry Maier Festival Park

Date_____

www.ingramcontent.com/pod-product-compliance
Lightning Source LLC
Chambersburg PA
CBHW050753090426

42736CB00004B/221